D0036224

"The best play of the year, bar none. *Doubt* is a great—let's repeat, *great*—new drama. Driven by strong conflict and crafted with subtlety, Shanley's writing is incisive, insightful and masterfully controlled. Taut, yet thoughtful, the writing is direct and swift as an arrow. This is enthralling theatre and should not be missed."

—Michael Sommers, *Newark Star-Ledger*

"*Doubt* may well be Shanley's best play to date."

—John Simon, *New York* Magazine

"#1 show of the year. A terrific, marvelous new play with astonishing theatricality. *Doubt* wakes up the slumbering theatre season, jolting the audience with a tough, timely story, rich in character, language and ideas. *Doubt* is Shanley's best play in years."

—Michael Kuchwara, *Associated Press*

"All the elements come invigoratingly together like clockwork in John Patrick Shanley's provocative new play, *Doubt*, a gripping story of suspicion cast on a priest's behavior that is less about scandal than about fascinatingly nuanced questions of moral certainty. Something rare for this season: a laudable new American play."

—David Rooney, *Variety*

"Compelling. The prolific Shanley folds doubts back upon each other in what may be his strongest script yet."

—Robert Hurwitt, *San Francisco Chronicle*

"One of the year's ten best. Moral certainty never seemed so suspect as in John Patrick Shanley's evocative and beautifully crafted thriller."

—David Cote, *TimeOut New York*

"A supremely intelligent new play. The must-see play of the season!"

—Jacques Le Sourd, *Journal News*, Westchester

"Riveting, exceptional theatre!"

—Liz Smith

Doubt

a parable

Doubt

a parable

John Patrick Shanley

THEATRE COMMUNICATIONS GROUP
NEW YORK

Doubt, a parable is published by Theatre Communications Group, Inc., 520 Eighth Avenue, 24th Floor, New York, NY 10018–4156.

This publication is made possible in part with public funds from the New York State Council on the Arts, a State Agency.

TCG books are exclusively distributed to the book trade by Consortium Book Sales and Distribution.

Library of Congress Cataloging-in-Publication Data
Shanley, John Patrick.
Doubt / John Patrick Shanley.
p. cm.
ISBN-13: 978-1-55936-276-4
ISBN-10: 1-55936-276-6
(pbk. : alk. paper)
1. Nuns—Drama. 2. Clergy—Drama. 3. Catholics—Drama.
4. Child sexual abuse—Drama.
I. Title.
PS3569.H3337D68 2005
812'.54—dc22   2005005284

Cover design by SPOTCO
Cover photo illustration by Marc Yankus
Author photo by Monique Carboni
Text design and composition by Lisa Govan

First Edition, April 2005
Fifteenth Printing, February 2013

This play is dedicated to the many orders of
Catholic nuns who have devoted their lives
to serving others in hospitals, schools
and retirement homes.
Though they have been much maligned and ridiculed,
who among us has been so generous?

———

Preface

What's under a play? What holds it up? You might as well ask what's under me? On what am I built? There's something silent under every person and under every play. There is something unsaid under any given society as well.

There's a symptom apparent in America right now. It's evident in political talk shows, in entertainment coverage, in artistic criticism of every kind, in religious discussion. We are living in a courtroom culture. We *were* living in a celebrity culture, but that's dead. Now we're only interested in celebrities if they're in court. We are living in a culture of extreme advocacy, of confrontation, of judgment, and of verdict. Discussion has given way to debate. Communication has become a contest of wills. Public talking has become obnoxious and insincere. Why? Maybe it's because deep down under the chatter we have come to a place where we know that we don't know . . . anything. But nobody's willing to say that.

Let me ask you. Have you ever held a position in an argument past the point of comfort? Have you ever defended a way of life you were on the verge of exhausting? Have you ever given service to a creed you no longer utterly believed? Have you ever told a girl you loved her and felt the faint nausea of eroding conviction? I have. That's an interesting moment. For a playwright, it's the beginning of an idea. I saw a piece of real estate on which I might build a play, a play that sat on something silent in my life and in my time. I started with a title: *Doubt*.

What is Doubt? Each of us is like a planet. There's the crust, which seems eternal. We are confident about who we are. If you ask, we can readily describe our current state. I know my answers to so many questions, as do you. What was your father like? Do you believe in God? Who's your best friend? What do you want? Your answers are your current topography, seemingly permanent, but deceptively so. Because under that face of easy response, there is another You. And this wordless Being moves just as the instant moves; it presses upward without explanation, fluid and wordless, until the resisting consciousness has no choice but to give way.

It is Doubt (so often experienced initially as weakness) that changes things. When a man feels unsteady, when he falters, when hard-won knowledge evaporates before his eyes, he's on the verge of growth. The subtle or violent reconciliation of the outer person and the inner core often seems at first like a mistake, like you've gone the wrong way and you're lost. But this is just emotion longing for the familiar. Life happens when the tectonic power of your speechless soul breaks through the dead habits of the mind. Doubt is nothing less than an opportunity to reenter the Present.

The play. I've set my story in 1964, when not just me, but the whole world seemed to be going through some kind of vast puberty. The old ways were still dominant in behavior, dress, morality, world view, but what had been organic expression had become a dead mask. I was in a Catholic church school in the Bronx, run by the Sisters of Charity. These women dressed in black, believed in Hell, obeyed their male counterparts, and educated us. The faith, which held us together, went beyond the precincts of religion. It was a shared dream we agreed to call Reality. We didn't know it, but we had a deal, a social contract. We would all believe the same thing. We would all believe.

Looking back, it seems to me, in those schools at that time, we were an ageless unity. We were all adults and we were all children. We had, like many animals, flocked together for warmth and safety. As a result, we were terribly vulnerable to anyone who chose to hunt us. When trust is the order of the day, predators are free to plunder. And plunder they did. As the ever widening Church scandals reveal, the hunters had a field day. And the shepherds, so invested in the surface, sacrificed actual good for perceived virtue.

I have never forgotten the lessons of that era, nor learned them well enough. I still long for a shared certainty, an assumption of safety, the reassurance of believing that others know better than me what's for the best. But I have been led by the bitter necessities of an interesting life to value that age-old practice of the wise: Doubt.

There is an uneasy time when belief has begun to slip, but hypocrisy has yet to take hold, when the consciousness is disturbed but not yet altered. It is the most dangerous, important, and ongoing experience of life. The beginning of change is the moment of Doubt. It is that crucial moment when I renew my humanity or become a lie.

Doubt requires more courage than conviction does, and more energy; because conviction is a resting place and doubt is infinite—it is a passionate exercise. You may come out of my play uncertain. You may want to be sure. Look down on that feeling. We've got to learn to live with a full measure of uncertainty. There is no last word. That's the silence under the chatter of our time.

John Patrick Shanley
Brooklyn, New York
March 2005

Doubt

a parable

Production History

Doubt, a parable received its world premiere at Manhattan Theatre Club (Lynne Meadow, Artistic Director; Barry Grove, Executive Producer) on November 23, 2004. The production then transferred to Broadway's Walter Kerr Theatre (Carole Shorenstein Hays; MTC Productions, Inc.; Roger Berlind; Scott Rudin; producers) and opened there on March 31, 2005. The production was directed by Doug Hughes; with scenic design by John Lee Beatty, costume design by Catherine Zuber, lighting design by Pat Collins and original music and sound design by David Van Tieghem. The production stage manager was Charles Means and the stage manager was Elizabeth Moloney. The cast was as follows:

FATHER FLYNN	Brían F. O'Byrne
SISTER ALOYSIUS	Cherry Jones
SISTER JAMES	Heather Goldenhersh
MRS. MULLER	Adriane Lenox

Characters

Setting

St. Nicholas, a Catholic church
and school in the Bronx, New York, 1964

The bad sleep well.

—Title of Kurosawa film

In much wisdom is much grief:
and he that increaseth knowledge increaseth sorrow.

—Ecclesiastes

Everything that is hard to attain
is easily assailed by the mob.

—Ptolemy

I

A priest, Father Flynn, in his late thirties, in green and gold vestments, gives a sermon. He is working class, from the Northeast.

FLYNN: What do you do when you're not sure? That's the topic of my sermon today. You look for God's direction and can't find it. Last year when President Kennedy was assassinated, who among us did not experience the most profound disorientation. Despair. "What now? Which way? What do I say to my kids? What do I tell myself?" It was a time of people sitting together, bound together by a common feeling of hopelessness. But think of that! Your *bond* with your fellow beings was your *despair*. It was a public experience, shared by everyone in our society. It was awful, but we were in it together! How much worse is it then for the lone man, the lone woman, stricken by a private calamity? "No one knows

I'm sick. No one knows I've lost my last real friend. No one knows I've done something wrong." Imagine the isolation. You see the world as through a window. On the one side of the glass: happy, untroubled people. On the other side: you. Something has happened, you have to carry it, and it's incommunicable. For those so afflicted, only God knows their pain. Their secret. The secret of their alienating sorrow. And when such a person, as they must, howls to the sky, to God: "Help me!" What if no answer comes? Silence. I want to tell you a story. A cargo ship sank and all her crew was drowned. Only this one sailor survived. He made a raft of some spars and, being of a nautical discipline, turned his eyes to the Heavens and read the stars. He set a course for his home, and, exhausted, fell asleep. Clouds rolled in and blanketed the sky. For the next twenty nights, as he floated on the vast ocean, he could no longer see the stars. He thought he was on course but there was no way to be certain. As the days rolled on, and he wasted away with fevers, thirst and starvation, he began to have doubts. Had he set his course right? Was he still going on towards his home? Or was he horribly lost and doomed to a terrible death? No way to know. The message of the constellations—had he imagined it because of his desperate circumstance? Or had he seen Truth once, and now had to hold on to it without further reassurance? That was his dilemma on a voyage without apparent end. There are those of you in church today who know exactly the crisis of faith I describe. I want to say to you: Doubt can be a bond as powerful and sustaining as certainty. When you are lost, you are not alone. In the name of the Father, the Son, and the Holy Ghost. Amen.

(He exits.)

II

The lights crossfade to a corner office in a Catholic school in the Bronx. The principal, Sister Aloysius Beauvier, sits at her desk, writing in a ledger with a fountain pen. She is in her fifties or sixties. She is watchful, reserved, unsentimental. She is of the order of the Sisters of Charity. She wears a black bonnet and floor-length black habit, rimless glasses. A knock at the door.

SISTER ALOYSIUS: Come in.

> *(Sister James, also of the Sisters of Charity, pokes her head in. She is in her twenties. There's a bit of sunshine in her heart, though she's reserved as well.)*

SISTER JAMES: Have you a moment, Sister Aloysius?
SISTER ALOYSIUS: Come in, Sister James.

> *(She enters.)*

Who's watching your class?
SISTER JAMES: They're having Art.
SISTER ALOYSIUS: Art. Waste of time.
SISTER JAMES: It's only an hour a week.
SISTER ALOYSIUS: Much can be accomplished in sixty minutes.
SISTER JAMES: Yes, Sister Aloysius. I wondered if I might know what you did about William London?
SISTER ALOYSIUS: I sent him home.
SISTER JAMES: Oh dear. So he's still bleeding?
SISTER ALOYSIUS: Oh yes.
SISTER JAMES: His nose just let loose and started gushing during The Pledge of Allegiance.
SISTER ALOYSIUS: Was it spontaneous?

SISTER JAMES: What else would it be?

SISTER ALOYSIUS: Self-induced.

SISTER JAMES: You mean, you think he might've intentionally given himself a nosebleed?

SISTER ALOYSIUS: Exactly.

SISTER JAMES: No!

SISTER ALOYSIUS: You are a very innocent person, Sister James. William London is a fidgety boy and if you do not keep right on him, he will do anything to escape his chair. He would set his foot on fire for half a day out of school.

SISTER JAMES: But why?

SISTER ALOYSIUS: He has a restless mind.

SISTER JAMES: But that's good.

SISTER ALOYSIUS: No, it's not. His father's a policeman and the last thing he wants is a rowdy boy. William London is headed for trouble. Puberty has got hold of him. He will be imagining all the wrong things, and I strongly suspect he will not graduate high school. But that's beyond our jurisdiction. We simply have to get him through, out the door, and then he's somebody else's project. Ordinarily, I assign my most experienced sisters to eighth grade but I'm working within constraints. Are you in control of your class?

SISTER JAMES: I think so.

SISTER ALOYSIUS: Usually more children are sent down to me.

SISTER JAMES: I try to take care of things myself.

SISTER ALOYSIUS: That can be an error. You are answerable to me, I to the monsignor, he to the bishop, and so on up to the Holy Father. There's a chain of discipline. Make use of it.

SISTER JAMES: Yes, Sister.

SISTER ALOYSIUS: How's Donald Muller doing?

SISTER JAMES: Steady.

SISTER ALOYSIUS: Good. Has anyone hit him?

SISTER JAMES: No.

SISTER ALOYSIUS: Good. That girl Linda Conte, have you seated her away from the boys?

SISTER JAMES: As far as space permits. It doesn't do much good.

SISTER ALOYSIUS: Just get her through. Intact.

(Pause. Sister Aloysius is staring absently at Sister James. A silence falls.)

SISTER JAMES: So. Should I go? *(No answer)* Is something the matter?

SISTER ALOYSIUS: No. Why? Is something the matter?

SISTER JAMES: I don't think so.

SISTER ALOYSIUS: Then nothing's the matter then.

SISTER JAMES: Well. Thank you, Sister. I just wanted to check on William's nose.

(She starts to go.)

SISTER ALOYSIUS: He had a ballpoint pen.

SISTER JAMES: Excuse me, Sister?

SISTER ALOYSIUS: William London had a ballpoint pen. He was fiddling with it while he waited for his mother. He's not using it for assignments, I hope.

SISTER JAMES: No, of course not.

SISTER ALOYSIUS: I'm sorry I allowed even cartridge pens into the school. The students really should only be learning script with true fountain pens. Always the easy way out these days. What does that teach? Every easy choice today will have its consequence tomorrow. Mark my words.

SISTER JAMES: Yes, Sister.

SISTER ALOYSIUS: Ballpoints make them press down, and when they press down, they write like monkeys.

SISTER JAMES: I don't allow them ballpoint pens.

SISTER ALOYSIUS: Good. Penmanship is dying all across the country. You have some time. Sit down.

(Sister James hesitates and sits down.)

We might as well have a talk. I've been meaning to talk to you. I observed your lesson on the New Deal at the beginning of the term. Not bad. But I caution you. Do not idealize Franklin Delano Roosevelt. He was a good president, but he did attempt to pack the Supreme Court. I do not approve of making heroes of lay historical figures. If you want to talk about saints, do it in Religion.

SISTER JAMES: Yes, Sister.

SISTER ALOYSIUS: Also. I question your enthusiasm for History.

SISTER JAMES: But I love History!

SISTER ALOYSIUS: That is exactly my meaning. You favor History and risk swaying the children to value it over their other subjects. I think this is a mistake.

SISTER JAMES: I never thought of that. I'll try to treat my other lessons with more enthusiasm.

SISTER ALOYSIUS: No. Give them their History without putting sugar all over it. That's the point. Now. Tell me about your class. How would you characterize the condition of 8-B?

SISTER JAMES: I don't know where to begin. What do you want to know?

SISTER ALOYSIUS: Let's begin with Stephen Inzio.

SISTER JAMES: Stephen Inzio has the highest marks in the class.

SISTER ALOYSIUS: Noreen Horan?

SISTER JAMES: Second highest marks.

SISTER ALOYSIUS: Brenda McNulty?

SISTER JAMES: Third highest.

SISTER ALOYSIUS: You see I am making a point, Sister James. I know that Stephen Inzio, Noreen Horan and Brenda McNulty are one, two and three in your class. School-wide, there are forty-eight such students each grade period. I make it my business to know all forty-eight of their names. I do not say this to aggrandize myself, but to illustrate the importance of paying attention. You must pay attention as well.

SISTER JAMES: Yes, Sister Aloysius.

SISTER ALOYSIUS: I cannot be everywhere.

SISTER JAMES: Am I falling short, Sister?

SISTER ALOYSIUS: These three students with the highest marks. Are they the most intelligent children in your class?

SISTER JAMES: No, I wouldn't say they are. But they work the hardest.

SISTER ALOYSIUS: Very good! That's right! That's the ethic. What good's a gift if it's left in the box? What good is a high IQ if you're staring out the window with your mouth agape? Be hard on the bright ones, Sister James. Don't be charmed by cleverness. Not theirs. And not yours. I think you are a competent teacher, Sister James, but maybe not our best teacher. The best teachers do not perform, they cause the students to perform.

SISTER JAMES: Do I perform?

SISTER ALOYSIUS: As if on a Broadway stage.

SISTER JAMES: Oh dear. I had no conception!

SISTER ALOYSIUS: You're showing off. You like to see yourself ten feet tall in their eyes. Another thing occurs to me. Where were you before?

SISTER JAMES: Mount St. Margaret's.

SISTER ALOYSIUS: All girls.

11

SISTER JAMES: Yes.

SISTER ALOYSIUS: I feel I must remind you. Boys are made of gravel, soot and tar paper. Boys are a different breed.

SISTER JAMES: I feel I know how to handle them.

SISTER ALOYSIUS: But perhaps you are wrong. And perhaps you are not working hard enough.

SISTER JAMES: Oh.

(Sister James cries a little.)

SISTER ALOYSIUS: No tears.

SISTER JAMES: I thought you were satisfied with me.

SISTER ALOYSIUS: Satisfaction is a vice. Do you have a hand-kerchief?

SISTER JAMES: Yes.

SISTER ALOYSIUS: Use it. Do you think that Socrates was sat-isfied? Good teachers are never content. We have some three hundred and seventy-two students in this school. It is a society which requires constant educational, spir-itual and human vigilance. I cannot afford an excessively innocent instructor in my eighth grade class. It's self-indulgent. Innocence is a form of laziness. Innocent teach-ers are easily duped. You must be canny, Sister James.

SISTER JAMES: Yes, Sister.

SISTER ALOYSIUS: When William London gets a nosebleed, be skeptical. Don't let a little blood fuddle your judg-ment. God gave you a brain and a heart. The heart is warm, but your wits must be cold. Liars should be frightened to lie to you. They should be uncomfortable in your presence. I doubt they are.

SISTER JAMES: I don't know. I've never thought about it.

SISTER ALOYSIUS: The children should think you see right through them.

SISTER JAMES: Wouldn't that be a little frightening?

SISTER ALOYSIUS: Only to the ones that are up to no good.

SISTER JAMES: But I want my students to feel they can talk to me.

SISTER ALOYSIUS: They're children. They can talk to each other. It's more important they have a fierce moral guardian. You stand at the door, Sister. You are the gatekeeper. If you are vigilant, they will not need to be.

SISTER JAMES: I'm not sure what you want me to do.

SISTER ALOYSIUS: And if things occur in your classroom which you sense require understanding, but you don't understand, come to me.

SISTER JAMES: Yes, Sister.

SISTER ALOYSIUS: That's why I'm here. That's why I'm the principal of this school. Do you stay when the specialty instructors come in?

SISTER JAMES: Yes.

SISTER ALOYSIUS: But you're here now while the Art class is going on.

SISTER JAMES: I was a little concerned about William's nose.

SISTER ALOYSIUS: Right. So you have Art in class.

SISTER JAMES: She comes in. Mrs. Bell. Yes.

SISTER ALOYSIUS: And you take them down to the basement for Dance with Mrs. Shields.

SISTER JAMES: On Thursdays.

SISTER ALOYSIUS: Another waste of time.

SISTER JAMES: Oh, but everyone loves the Christmas pageant.

SISTER ALOYSIUS: I don't love it. Frankly it offends me. Last year the girl playing Our Lady was wearing lipstick. I was waiting in the wings for that little jade.

SISTER JAMES: Then there's Music.

SISTER ALOYSIUS: That strange woman with the portable piano. What's wrong with her neck?

SISTER JAMES: Some kind of goiter. Poor woman.

SISTER ALOYSIUS: Yes. Mrs. Carolyn.

SISTER JAMES: That's right.

SISTER ALOYSIUS: We used to have a Sister teaching that. Not enough Sisters. What else?

SISTER JAMES: Physical Education and Religion.

SISTER ALOYSIUS: And for that we have Father Flynn. Two hours a week. And you stay for those?

SISTER JAMES: Mostly. Unless I have reports to fill out or . . .

SISTER ALOYSIUS: What do you think of Father Flynn?

SISTER JAMES: Oh, he's a brilliant man. What a speaker!

SISTER ALOYSIUS: Yes. His sermon this past Sunday was poetic.

SISTER JAMES: He's actually very good, too, at teaching basketball. I was surprised. I wouldn't think a man of the cloth the personality type for basketball, but he has a way he has, very natural with dribbling and shooting.

SISTER ALOYSIUS: What do you think that sermon was about?

SISTER JAMES: What?

SISTER ALOYSIUS: This past Sunday. What was he talking about?

SISTER JAMES: Well, Doubt. He was talking about Doubt.

SISTER ALOYSIUS: Why?

SISTER JAMES: Excuse me, Sister?

SISTER ALOYSIUS: Well, sermons come from somewhere, don't they? Is Father Flynn in Doubt, is he concerned that someone else is in Doubt?

SISTER JAMES: I suppose you'd have to ask him.

SISTER ALOYSIUS: No. That would not be appropriate. He is my superior. And if he were troubled, he should confess it to a fellow priest, or the monsignor. We do not share intimate information with priests.

(A pause.)

SISTER JAMES: I'm a little concerned.

(Sister Aloysius leans forward.)

SISTER ALOYSIUS: About what?

SISTER JAMES: The time. Art class will be over in a few minutes. I should go up.

SISTER ALOYSIUS: Have you noticed anything, Sister James?

SISTER JAMES: About what?

SISTER ALOYSIUS: I want you to be alert.

SISTER JAMES: I don't believe I'm following you, Sister.

SISTER ALOYSIUS: I'm sorry I'm not more forthright, but I must be careful not to create something by saying it. I can only say I am concerned, perhaps needlessly, about matters in St. Nicholas School.

SISTER JAMES: Academically?

SISTER ALOYSIUS: I wasn't inviting a guessing game. I want you to pay attention to your class.

SISTER JAMES: Well, of course I'll pay attention to my class, Sister. And I'll try not to perform. And I'll try to be less innocent. I'm sorry you're disappointed in me. Please know that I will try my best. Honestly.

SISTER ALOYSIUS: Look at you. You'd trade anything for a warm look. I'm telling you here and now, I want to see the starch in your character cultivated. If you are looking for reassurance, you can be fooled. If you forget yourself and study others, you will not be fooled. It's important. One final matter and then you really must get back. Sister Veronica is going blind.

SISTER JAMES: Oh how horrible!

SISTER ALOYSIUS: This is not generally known and I don't want it known. If they find out in the rectory, she'll be gone. I cannot afford to lose her. But now if you see her making her way down those stone stairs into the courtyard, for the love of Heaven, lightly take her hand as if in fellowship and see that she doesn't destroy herself. All right, go.

III

The lights crossfade to Father Flynn, whistle around his neck, in a sweatshirt and pants, holding a basketball.

FLYNN: All right, settle down, boys. Now the thing about shooting from the foul line: It's psychological. The rest of the game you're cooperating with your teammates, you're competing against the other team. But at the foul line, it's you against yourself. And the danger is: You start to think. When you think, you stop breathing. Your body locks up. So you have to remember to relax. Take a breath, unlock your knees—this is something for you to watch, Jimmy. You stand like a parking meter. Come up with a routine of what you do. Shift your weight, move your hips . . . You think that's funny, Ralph? What's funny is you never getting a foul shot. Don't worry if you look silly. They won't think you're silly if you get the basket. Come up with a routine, concentrate on the routine, and you'll forget to get tensed up. Now on another matter, I've noticed several of you guys have dirty nails. I don't want to see that. I'm not talking about the length of your nails, I'm talking about cleanliness. See? Look at my nails. They're long, I like them a little long, but look at how clean they are. That makes it okay. There was a kid I grew up with, Timmy Mathisson, never had clean nails, and he'd stick his fingers up his nose, in his mouth. —This is a true story, learn to listen! He got spinal meningitis and died a horrible death. Sometimes it's the little things that get you. You try to talk to a girl with those filthy paws, Mr. Conroy, she's gonna take off like she's being chased by the Red Chinese! *(Reacting genially to laughter)* All right, all right. You guys, what am I gonna do with you? Get dressed, come on over to the rectory, have some Kool-Aid and cookies, we'll have a bull session. *(Blows his whistle)* Go!

IV

Crossfade to a bit of garden, a bench, brick walls. Sister Aloysius, in full habit and a black shawl, is wrapping a pruned rosebush in burlap. Sister James enters.

SISTER JAMES: Good afternoon, Sister.
SISTER ALOYSIUS: Good afternoon, Sister James. Mr. McGinn pruned this bush, which was the right thing to do, but he neglected to protect it from the frost.
SISTER JAMES: Have we had a frost?
SISTER ALOYSIUS: When it comes, it's too late.
SISTER JAMES: You know about gardening?
SISTER ALOYSIUS: A little. Where is your class?
SISTER JAMES: The girls are having Music.
SISTER ALOYSIUS: And the boys?
SISTER JAMES: They're in the rectory.

(Sister James indicates the rectory, which is out of view, just on the other side of the garden.)

SISTER ALOYSIUS: With Father Flynn.
SISTER JAMES: Yes. He's giving them a talk.
SISTER ALOYSIUS: On what subject?

SISTER JAMES: How to be a man.

SISTER ALOYSIUS: Well, if Sisters were permitted in the rectory, I would be interested to hear that talk. I don't know how to be a man. I would like to know what's involved. Have you ever given the girls a talk on how to be a woman?

SISTER JAMES: No. I wouldn't be competent.

SISTER ALOYSIUS: Why not?

SISTER JAMES: I just don't think I would. I took my vows at the beginning . . . Before . . . At the beginning.

SISTER ALOYSIUS: The founder of our order, The Blessed Mother Seton, was married and had five children before embarking on her vows.

SISTER JAMES: I've often wondered how she managed so much in one life.

SISTER ALOYSIUS: Life perhaps is longer than you think and the dictates of the soul more numerous. I was married.

SISTER JAMES: You were!

(Sister Aloysius smiles for the first time.)

SISTER ALOYSIUS: You could at least hide your astonishment.

SISTER JAMES: I . . . didn't know.

SISTER ALOYSIUS: When one takes on the habit, one must close the door on secular things. My husband died in the war against Adolph Hitler.

SISTER JAMES: Really! Excuse me, Sister.

SISTER ALOYSIUS: But I'm like you. I'm not sure I would feel competent to lecture tittering girls on the subject of womanhood. I don't come into this garden often. What is it, forty feet across? The convent here, the rectory there. We might as well be separated by the Atlantic Ocean. I used to potter around out here, but Monsignor Benedict does his reverie at quixotic times and we are rightly discouraged from crossing paths with priests unattended. He is seventy-nine, but nevertheless.

SISTER JAMES: The monsignor is very good, isn't he?

SISTER ALOYSIUS: Yes. But he is oblivious.

SISTER JAMES: To what?

SISTER ALOYSIUS: I don't believe he knows who's President of the United States. I mean him no disrespect of course. It's just that he's otherworldly in the extreme.

SISTER JAMES: Is it that he's innocent, Sister Aloysius?

SISTER ALOYSIUS: You have a slyness at work, Sister James. Be careful of it. How is your class? How is Donald Muller?

SISTER JAMES: He is thirteenth in class.

SISTER ALOYSIUS: I know. That's sufficient. Is he being accepted?

SISTER JAMES: He has no friends.

SISTER ALOYSIUS: That would be a lot to expect after only two months. Has anyone hit him?

SISTER JAMES: No.

SISTER ALOYSIUS: Someone will. And when it happens, send them right down to me.

SISTER JAMES: I'm not so sure anyone will.

SISTER ALOYSIUS: There is a statue of St. Patrick on one side of the church altar and a statue of St. Anthony on the other. This parish serves Irish and Italian families. Someone will hit Donald Muller.

SISTER JAMES: He has a protector.

SISTER ALOYSIUS: Who?

SISTER JAMES: Father Flynn.

(Sister Aloysius, who has been fussing with mulch, is suddenly rigid. She rises.)

SISTER ALOYSIUS: What?

SISTER JAMES: He's taken an interest. Since Donald went on the altar boys. *(Pause)* I thought I should tell you.

SISTER ALOYSIUS: I told you to come to me, but I hoped you never would.

SISTER JAMES: Maybe I shouldn't have.

SISTER ALOYSIUS: I knew once you did, something would be set in motion. So it's happened.

SISTER JAMES: What?! I'm not telling you that! I'm not even certain what you mean.

SISTER ALOYSIUS: Yes, you are.

SISTER JAMES: I've been trying to become more cold in my thinking as you suggested . . . I feel as if I've lost my way a little, Sister Aloysius. I had the most terrible dream last night. I want to be guided by you and responsible to the children, but I want my peace of mind. I must tell you I have been longing for the return of my peace of mind.

SISTER ALOYSIUS: You may not have it. It is not your place to be complacent. That's for the children. That's what we give them.

SISTER JAMES: I think I'm starting to understand you a little. But it's so unsettling to look at things and people with suspicion. It feels as if I'm less close God.

SISTER ALOYSIUS: When you take a step to address wrong-doing, you are taking a step away from God, but in His service. Dealing with such matters is hard and thankless work.

SISTER JAMES: I've become more reserved in class. I feel separated from the children.

SISTER ALOYSIUS: That's as it should be.

SISTER JAMES: But I feel. Wrong. And about this other matter, I don't have any evidence. I'm not at all certain that anything's happened.

SISTER ALOYSIUS: We can't wait for that.

SISTER JAMES: But what if it's nothing?

SISTER ALOYSIUS: Then it's nothing. I wouldn't mind being wrong. But I doubt I am.

SISTER JAMES: Then what's to be done?

SISTER ALOYSIUS: I don't know.

SISTER JAMES: You'll know what to do.

SISTER ALOYSIUS: I don't know what to do. There are parameters which protect him and hinder me.

SISTER JAMES: But he can't be safe if it's established. I doubt he could recover from the shame.

SISTER ALOYSIUS: What have you seen?

SISTER JAMES: I don't know.

SISTER ALOYSIUS: What have you seen?

SISTER JAMES: He took Donald to the rectory.

SISTER ALOYSIUS: What for?

SISTER JAMES: A talk.

SISTER ALOYSIUS: Alone?

SISTER JAMES: Yes.

SISTER ALOYSIUS: When?

SISTER JAMES: A week ago.

SISTER ALOYSIUS: Why didn't you tell me?

SISTER JAMES: I didn't think there was anything wrong with it. It never came into my mind that he . . . that there could be anything wrong.

SISTER ALOYSIUS: Of all the children. Donald Muller. I suppose it makes sense.

SISTER JAMES: How does it make sense?

SISTER ALOYSIUS: He's isolated. The little sheep lagging behind is the one the wolf goes for.

SISTER JAMES: I don't know that anything's wrong!

SISTER ALOYSIUS: Our first Negro student. I thought there'd be fighting, a parent or two to deal with . . . I should've foreseen this possibility.

SISTER JAMES: How could you imagine it?

SISTER ALOYSIUS: It is my job to outshine the fox in cleverness! That's my job!

SISTER JAMES: But maybe it's nothing!

SISTER ALOYSIUS: Then why do you look like you've seen the Devil?

SISTER JAMES: It's just the way the boy acted when he came back to class.

SISTER ALOYSIUS: He said something?

SISTER JAMES: No. It was his expression. He looked frightened and . . . he put his head on the desk in the most peculiar way. *(Struggles)* And one other thing. I think there was alcohol on his breath. There was alcohol on his breath.

(Sister Aloysius looks toward the rectory.)

SISTER ALOYSIUS: Eight years ago at St. Boniface we had a priest who had to be stopped. But I had Monsignor Scully then . . . whom I could rely on. Here, there's no man I can go to, and men run everything. We are going to have to stop him ourselves.

SISTER JAMES: Can't you just . . . report your suspicions?

SISTER ALOYSIUS: To Monsignor Benedict? The man's guileless! He would just ask Father Flynn!

SISTER JAMES: Well, would that be such a bad idea?

SISTER ALOYSIUS: And he would believe whatever Father Flynn told him. He would think the matter settled.

SISTER JAMES: But maybe that is all that needs to be done. If it's true. If I had done something awful, and I was confronted with it, I'd be so repentant.

SISTER ALOYSIUS: Sister James, my dear, you must try to imagine a very different kind of person than yourself. A man who would do this has already denied a great deal. If I tell the monsignor and he is satisfied with Father Flynn's rebuttal, the matter is suppressed.

SISTER JAMES: Well then tell the bishop.

SISTER ALOYSIUS: The hierarchy of the Church does not permit my going to the bishop. No. Once I tell the monsignor, it's out of my hands, I'm helpless. I'm going to have to come up with a pretext, get Father Flynn into my office. Try to force it. You'll have to be there.

SISTER JAMES: Me? No! Why? Oh no, Sister! I couldn't!

SISTER ALOYSIUS: I can't be closeted alone with a priest. Another Sister must be in attendance and it has to be you. The circle of confidence mustn't be made any wider. Think of the boy if this gets out.

SISTER JAMES: I can't do it!

SISTER ALOYSIUS: Why not? You're squeamish?

SISTER JAMES: I'm not equipped! It's . . . I would be embarrassed. I couldn't possibly be present if the topic were spoken of!

SISTER ALOYSIUS: Please, Sister, do not indulge yourself in witless adolescent scruples. I assure you I would prefer a more seasoned confederate. But you are the one who came to me.

SISTER JAMES: You told me to!

SISTER ALOYSIUS: Would you rather leave the boy to be exploited? And don't think this will be the only story. If you close your eyes, you will be a party to all that comes after.

SISTER JAMES: You're supposed to tell the monsignor!

SISTER ALOYSIUS: That you saw a look in a boy's eye? That *perhaps* you smelled something on his breath? Monsignor Benedict thinks the sun rises and sets on Father Flynn. You'd be branded an hysteric and transferred.

SISTER JAMES: We can ask him.

SISTER ALOYSIUS: Who?

SISTER JAMES: The boy. Donald Muller.

SISTER ALOYSIUS: He'll deny it.

SISTER JAMES: Why?

SISTER ALOYSIUS: Shame.

SISTER JAMES: You can't know that.

SISTER ALOYSIUS: And if he does point the finger, how do you think that will be received in this community? A black child. *(No answer)* I am going to think this through. Then I'm going to invite Father Flynn to my office on an unrelated matter. You will be there.

SISTER JAMES: But what good can I do?

SISTER ALOYSIUS: Aside from the unacceptability of a priest and nun being alone, I need a witness.

SISTER JAMES: To what?

SISTER ALOYSIUS: He may tell the truth and lie afterwards.

(Sister James looks toward the rectory.)

SISTER JAMES: The boys are coming out of the rectory. They look happy enough.

SISTER ALOYSIUS: They look smug. Like they have a secret.

SISTER JAMES: There he is.

SISTER ALOYSIUS: If I could, Sister James, I would certainly choose to live in innocence. But innocence can only be wisdom in a world without evil. Situations arise and we are confronted with wrongdoing and the need to act.

SISTER JAMES: I have to take the boys up to class.

SISTER ALOYSIUS: Go on, then. Take them. I will be talking to you.

(The sound of wind. Sister Aloysius pulls her shawl tightly about her and goes. After a moment, Sister James goes as well.)

V

The principal's office. A phone rings. Sister Aloysius enters with a pot of tea, walking quickly to answer the phone.

SISTER ALOYSIUS: Hello, St. Nicholas School? Oh yes, Mr. McGinn. Thank you for calling back. That was quite a windstorm we had last night. No, I didn't know there was a Great Wind in Ireland and you were there for it. That's fascinating. Yes. I was wondering if you would be so kind as to remove a tree limb that's fallen in the courtyard of the church. Sister Veronica tripped on it this morning and fell on her face. I think she's all right. She doesn't look any worse, Mr. McGinn. Thank you, Mr. McGinn.

(She hangs up the phone and looks at her watch, a bit anxious. A knock at the door.)

Come in.

(The door opens. Father Flynn is standing there in his black cassock. He doesn't come in.)

FLYNN: Good morning, Sister Aloysius! How are you today?
SISTER ALOYSIUS: Good morning, Father Flynn. Very well. Good of you to come by.

(Father Flynn takes a step into the office.)

FLYNN: Are we ready for the meeting?
SISTER ALOYSIUS: We're just short Sister James. *(Father Flynn steps back into the doorway)* Did you hear that wind last night?

FLYNN: I certainly did. Imagine what it must've been like in the frontier days when a man alone in the woods sat by a fire in his buckskins and listened to a sound like that. Imagine the loneliness! The immense darkness pressing in! How frightening it must've been!

SISTER ALOYSIUS: If one lacked faith in God's protection, I suppose it would be frightening.

FLYNN: Did I hear Sister Veronica had an accident?

SISTER ALOYSIUS: Yes. Sister Veronica fell on a piece of wood this morning and practically killed herself.

FLYNN: Is she all right?

SISTER ALOYSIUS: Oh, she's fine.

FLYNN: Her sight isn't good, is it?

SISTER ALOYSIUS: Her sight is fine. Nuns fall, you know.

FLYNN: No, I didn't know that.

SISTER ALOYSIUS: It's the habit. It catches us up more often than not. What with our being in black and white, and so prone to falling, we're more like dominos than anything else.

(Sister James appears at the door, breathless.)

SISTER JAMES: Am I past the time?

(Father Flynn takes a step into the office.)

FLYNN: Not at all. Sister Aloysius and I were just having a nice chat.

SISTER JAMES: Good morning, Father Flynn. Good morning, Sister. I'm sorry I was delayed. Mr. McGinn has closed the courtyard to fix something so I had to go back through the convent and out the side door and then I ran into Sister Veronica.

FLYNN: How is she?

SISTER JAMES: She has a bit of a bloody nose.

SISTER ALOYSIUS: I'm beginning to think you're punching people.

SISTER JAMES: Sister?

SISTER ALOYSIUS: Well, after the incident with . . . Never mind. Well, come in, please. Sit down.

(They come in and sit down. Father Flynn takes Sister Aloysius's chair. He's sitting at her desk. She reacts, but says nothing.)

I actually have a hot pot of tea. *(Closes the door but for an inch)* And close this but not quite for form's sake. Would you have a cup of tea, Father?

FLYNN: I would love a cup of tea.

SISTER ALOYSIUS: Perhaps you could serve him, Sister?

SISTER JAMES: Of course.

SISTER ALOYSIUS: And yourself of course.

SISTER JAMES: Would you like tea, Sister Aloysius?

SISTER ALOYSIUS: I've already had my cup.

FLYNN: Is there sugar?

SISTER ALOYSIUS: Sugar? Yes! *(Rummages in her desk)* It's here somewhere. I put it in the drawer for Lent last year and never remembered to take it out.

FLYNN: It mustn't have been much to give up then.

SISTER ALOYSIUS: No, I'm sure you're right. Here it is. I'll serve you, though for want of practice, I'm . . . *(Clumsy)*

(She's got the sugar bowl and is poised to serve him a lump of sugar with a small pair of tongs when she sees his nails.)

Your fingernails.

FLYNN: I wear them a little long. The sugar?

SISTER ALOYSIUS: Oh yes. One?

FLYNN: Three.

SISTER ALOYSIUS: Three.

(She's appalled but tries to hide it.)

FLYNN: Sweet tooth.

SISTER ALOYSIUS: One, two, three. Sister, do you take sugar?

(Sister Aloysius looks at Sister James.)

SISTER JAMES *(To Sister Aloysius)*: Never! *(To Father Flynn)* Not that there's anything wrong with sugar. *(To Sister Aloysius again)* Thank you.

(Sister Aloysius puts the sugar away in her desk.)

SISTER ALOYSIUS: Well, thank you, Father, for making the time for us. We're at our wit's end.

FLYNN: I think it's an excellent idea to rethink the Christmas pageant. Last year's effort was a little woebegone.

SISTER JAMES: No! I loved it! *(Becomes self-conscious)* But I love all Christmas pageants. I just love the Nativity. The birth of the Savior. And the hymns of course. "O Little Town of Bethlehem," "O Come, O Come Emmanuel" . . .

SISTER ALOYSIUS: Thank you, Sister James. Sister James will be co-directing the pageant with Mrs. Shields this year. So what do you think, Father Flynn? Is there something new we could do?

FLYNN: Well, we all love the Christmas hymns, but it might be jolly to include a secular song.

SISTER ALOYSIUS: Secular.

FLYNN: Yes. "It's Beginning to Look a Lot Like Christmas." Something like that.

SISTER ALOYSIUS: What would be the point of performing a secular song?

FLYNN: Fun.

SISTER JAMES: Or "Frosty the Snowman."

FLYNN: That's a good one. We could have one of the boys dress as a snowman and dance around.

SISTER ALOYSIUS: Which boy?

FLYNN: We'd do tryouts.

SISTER ALOYSIUS: "Frosty the Snowman" espouses a pagan belief in magic. The snowman comes to life when an enchanted hat is put on his head. If the music were more somber, people would realize the images are disturbing and the song heretical.

(Sister James and Father Flynn exchange a look.)

SISTER JAMES: I've never thought about "Frosty the Snowman" like that.

SISTER ALOYSIUS: It should be banned from the airwaves.

FLYNN: So. Not "Frosty the Snowman."

(Father Flynn writes something in a small notebook.)

SISTER ALOYSIUS: I don't think so. "It's Beginning to Look a Lot Like Christmas" would be fine I suppose. The parents would like it. May I ask what you wrote down? With that ballpoint pen.

FLYNN: Oh. Nothing. An idea for a sermon.

SISTER ALOYSIUS: You had one just now?

FLYNN: I get them all the time.

SISTER ALOYSIUS: How fortunate.

FLYNN: I forget them so I write them down.

SISTER ALOYSIUS: What is the idea?

FLYNN: Intolerance.

(Sister James tries to break a bit of tension.)

SISTER JAMES: Would you like a little more tea, Father?

FLYNN: Not yet. I think a message of the Second Ecumenical Council was that the Church needs to take on a more familiar face. Reflect the local community. We should sing a song from the radio now and then. Take the kids out for ice cream.

SISTER ALOYSIUS: Ice cream.

FLYNN: Maybe take the boys on a camping trip. We should be friendlier. The children and the parents should see us as members of their family rather than emissaries from Rome. I think the pageant should be charming, like a community theatre doing a show.

SISTER ALOYSIUS: But we are not members of their family. We're different.

FLYNN: Why? Because of our vows?

SISTER ALOYSIUS: Precisely.

FLYNN: I don't think we're so different. *(To Sister James)* You know, I would take some more tea, Sister. Thank you.

SISTER ALOYSIUS: And they think we're different. The working-class people of this parish trust us to be different.

FLYNN: I think we're getting off the subject.

SISTER ALOYSIUS: Yes, you're right, back to it. The Christmas pageant. We must be careful how Donald Muller is used in the pageant.

(Sister James shakes as she pours the tea.)

FLYNN: Easy there, Sister, you don't spill.

SISTER JAMES: Oh, uh, yes, Father.

FLYNN: What about Donald Muller?

SISTER ALOYSIUS: We must be careful, in the pageant, that we neither hide Donald Muller nor put him forward.

FLYNN: Because of the color of his skin.

SISTER ALOYSIUS: That's right.

FLYNN: Why?

SISTER ALOYSIUS: Come, Father. You're being disingenuous.

FLYNN: I think he should be treated like every other boy.

SISTER ALOYSIUS: You yourself singled the boy out for special attention. You held a private meeting with him at the rectory. *(Turning to Sister James)* A week ago?

SISTER JAMES: Yes.

(He realizes something's up.)

FLYNN: What are we talking about?

SISTER JAMES: Donald Muller?

SISTER ALOYSIUS: The boy acted strangely when he returned to class.

(Father Flynn turns to Sister James.)

FLYNN: He did?

SISTER JAMES: When he returned from the rectory. A little odd, yes.

SISTER ALOYSIUS: Can you tell us why?

FLYNN: How did he act strangely?

SISTER JAMES: I'm not sure how to explain it. He laid his head on the desk . . .

FLYNN: You mean you had some impression?

SISTER JAMES: Yes.

FLYNN: And he'd come from the rectory so you're asking me if I know anything about it?

SISTER JAMES: That's it.

FLYNN: Hmmm. Did you want to discuss the pageant, is that why I'm here, or is this what you wanted to discuss?

SISTER ALOYSIUS: This.

FLYNN: Well. I feel a little uncomfortable.

SISTER ALOYSIUS: Why?

FLYNN: Why do you think? Something about your tone.

SISTER ALOYSIUS: I would prefer a discussion of fact rather than tone.

FLYNN: Well. If I had judged my conversation with Donald Muller to be of concern to you, Sister, I would have sat you down and talked to you about it. But I did not judge it to be of concern to you.

SISTER ALOYSIUS: Perhaps you are mistaken in your understanding of what concerns me. The boy is in my school and his well-being is my responsibility.

FLYNN: His well-being is not at issue.

SISTER ALOYSIUS: I am not satisfied that that is true. He was upset when he returned to class.

FLYNN: Did he say something?

SISTER JAMES: No.

SISTER ALOYSIUS: What happened in the rectory?

FLYNN: Happened? Nothing happened. I had a talk with a boy.

SISTER ALOYSIUS: What about?

FLYNN: It was a private matter.

SISTER ALOYSIUS: He's twelve years old. What could be private?

FLYNN: I'll say it again, Sister. I object to your tone.

SISTER ALOYSIUS: This is not about my tone or your tone, Father Flynn. It's about arriving at the truth.

FLYNN: Of what?

SISTER ALOYSIUS: You know what I'm talking about. Don't you? You're controlling the expression on your face right now. Aren't you?

FLYNN: My face? You said you wanted to talk about the pageant, Sister. That's why I'm here. Am I to understand that you brought me into your office to confront me in some way? It's outrageous. I'm not answerable to you. What exactly are you accusing me of?

SISTER ALOYSIUS: I am not accusing you of anything, Father Flynn. I am asking you to tell me what happened in the rectory.

(Father Flynn stands.)

FLYNN: I don't wish to continue this conversation at all further. And if you are dissatisfied with that, I suggest you speak to Monsignor Benedict. I can only imagine that your unfortunate behavior this morning is the result of overwork. Perhaps you need a leave of absence. I may suggest it. Have a good morning. *(To Sister James)* Sister?

SISTER JAMES: Good morning, Father.

(Sister Aloysius's next words stop him.)

SISTER ALOYSIUS: There was alcohol on his breath. *(He turns)* When he returned from his meeting with you.

(He comes back and sits down. He rubs his eyes.)

FLYNN: Alcohol.

SISTER JAMES: I did smell it on his breath.

SISTER ALOYSIUS: Well?

FLYNN: Can't you let this alone?

SISTER ALOYSIUS: No.

FLYNN: I see there's no way out of this.

SISTER JAMES: Take your time, Father. Would you like some more tea?

FLYNN: You should've let it alone.

SISTER ALOYSIUS: Not possible.

FLYNN: Donald Muller served as altar boy last Tuesday morning. After Mass, Mr. McGinn caught him in the sacristy drinking altar wine. When I found out, I sent for him.

There were tears. He begged not to be removed from the altar boys. And I took pity on him. I told him if no one else found out, I would let him stay on.

(Sister James is overjoyed. Sister Aloysius is unmoved.)

SISTER JAMES: Oh, what a relief! That explains everything! Thanks be to God! Oh, Sister, look, it's all a mistake!

SISTER ALOYSIUS: And if I talk to Mr. McGinn?

FLYNN: Talk to Mr. McGinn by all means. But now that the boy's secret's out, I'm going to have to remove him from the altar boys. Which I think is too bad. That's what I was trying to avoid.

SISTER JAMES: You were trying to protect the boy!

FLYNN: That's right.

SISTER JAMES: I might've done the same thing! *(To Sister Aloysius)* Is there a way Donald could stay on the altar boys?

SISTER ALOYSIUS: No. If the boy drank altar wine, he cannot continue as an altar boy.

FLYNN: Of course you're right. I'm just not the disciplinarian you are, Sister. And he is the only Negro in the school. That did affect my thinking on the matter. It will be commented on that he's no longer serving at Mass. It's a public thing. A certain ignorant element in the parish will be confirmed in their beliefs.

SISTER ALOYSIUS: He must be held to the same standard as the others.

FLYNN: Of course. Do we need to discuss the pageant or was that just . . .

SISTER ALOYSIUS: No, this was the issue.

FLYNN: Are you satisfied?

SISTER ALOYSIUS: Yes.

FLYNN: Then I'll be going. I have some writing to do.

SISTER ALOYSIUS: Intolerance.

FLYNN: That's right.

(*He goes, then stops at the door.*)

I'm not pleased with how you handled this, Sister. Next time you are troubled by dark ideas, I suggest you speak to the monsignor.

(*He goes. After a moment, Sister James weakly launches into optimism.*)

SISTER JAMES: Well. What a relief! He cleared it all up.

SISTER ALOYSIUS: You believe him?

SISTER JAMES: Of course.

SISTER ALOYSIUS: Isn't it more that it's easier to believe him?

SISTER JAMES: But we can corroborate his story with Mr. McGinn!

SISTER ALOYSIUS: Yes. These types of people are clever. They're not so easily undone.

SISTER JAMES: Well, I'm convinced!

SISTER ALOYSIUS: You're not. You just want things to be resolved so you can have simplicity back.

SISTER JAMES: I want no further part of this.

SISTER ALOYSIUS: I'll bring him down. With or without your help.

SISTER JAMES: How can you be so sure he's lying?

SISTER ALOYSIUS: Experience.

SISTER JAMES: You just don't like him! You don't like it that he uses a ballpoint pen. You don't like it that he takes three lumps of sugar in his tea. You don't like it that he likes "Frosty the Snowman." And you're letting that convince you of something terrible, just terrible! Well, I like "Frosty the Snowman"! And it would be nice if this school weren't run like a prison! And I think it's a good thing that I love to teach History and that I might inspire my students to love it, too! And if you judge that to mean I'm not fit to be a teacher, then so be it!

SISTER ALOYSIUS: Sit down. *(Sister James does)* In ancient Sparta, important matters were decided by who shouted loudest. Fortunately, we are not in ancient Sparta. Now. Do you honestly find the students in this school to be treated like inmates in a prison?

SISTER JAMES *(Relenting)*: No, I don't. Actually, by and large, they seem to be fairly happy. But they're all uniformly terrified of you!

SISTER ALOYSIUS: Yes. That's how it works. Sit there.

(Sister Aloysius looks in a notebook, picks up the phone, dials.)

Hello, this is Sister Aloysius Beauvier, the principal of St. Nicholas. Is this Mrs. Muller? I'm calling about your son, Donald. I would like you and your husband to come down here for a talk. When would be convenient?

(Lights fade.)

VI

Father Flynn, in blue and white vestments, is at the pulpit.

FLYNN: A woman was gossiping with a friend about a man she hardly knew—I know none of you have ever done this—and that night she had a dream. A great hand appeared over her and pointed down at her. She was immediately seized with an overwhelming sense of guilt. The next day she went to confession. She got the old parish priest, Father O'Rourke, and she told him the whole thing. "Is gossiping a sin?" she asked the old man. "Was that the Hand of God Almighty pointing a finger at me? Should I be asking your absolution? Father, tell me, have I done something wrong?" *(Irish brogue)* "Yes!" Father O'Rourke answered her. "Yes, you ignorant, badly brought-up female! You have borne false witness against your neighbor, you have played fast and loose with his reputation, and you should be heartily ashamed!" So the woman said she was sorry and asked forgiveness. "Not so fast!" says O'Rourke. "I want you to go home, take a pillow up on your roof, cut it open with a knife, and return here to me!" So she went home, took the pillow off her bed, a knife from the drawer, went up the fire escape to the roof, and stabbed the pillow. Then she went back to the old priest as instructed. "Did you gut the pillow with the knife?" he says. "Yes, Father." "And what was the result?" "Feathers," she said. "Feathers"? he repeated. "Feathers everywhere, Father!" "Now I want you to go back and gather up every last feather that flew out on the wind!" "Well," she says, "it can't be done. I don't know where they went. The wind took them all over." "And that," said Father O'Rourke, "is *gossip*!" In the name of the Father, Son, and the Holy Ghost, Amen.

VII

*The lights crossfade to the garden. A crow caws. Sister James
sits on the bench, deep in thought. Father Flynn enters.*

FLYNN: Good afternoon, Sister James.

SISTER JAMES: Good afternoon, Father.

FLYNN: What is that bird complaining about? What kind of
bird is that? A starling? A grackle?

SISTER JAMES: A crow?

FLYNN: Of course it is. Are you praying? I didn't mean to
interrupt.

SISTER JAMES: I'm not praying, no.

FLYNN: You seem subdued.

SISTER JAMES: Oh. I can't sleep.

FLYNN: Why not?

SISTER JAMES: Bad dreams. Actually one bad dream, and
then I haven't slept right since.

FLYNN: What about?

SISTER JAMES: I looked in a mirror and there was a darkness
where my face should be. It frightened me.

FLYNN: I can't sleep on occasion.

SISTER JAMES: No? Do you see that big hand pointing a finger at you?

FLYNN: Yes. Sometimes.

SISTER JAMES: Was your sermon directed at anyone in
particular?

FLYNN: What do you think?

SISTER JAMES: Did you make up that story about the pillow?

FLYNN: Yes. You make up little stories to illustrate. In the tra-
dition of the parable.

SISTER JAMES: Aren't the things that actually happen in life
more worthy of interpretation than a made-up story?

FLYNN: No. What actually happens in life is beyond interpretation. The truth makes for a bad sermon. It tends to be confusing and have no clear conclusion.

SISTER JAMES: I received a letter from my brother in Maryland yesterday. He's very sick.

FLYNN: Maybe you should go and see him.

SISTER JAMES: I can't leave my class.

FLYNN: How's Donald Muller doing?

SISTER JAMES: I don't know.

FLYNN: You don't see him?

SISTER JAMES: I see him every day, but I don't know how he's doing. I don't know how to judge these things. Now.

FLYNN: I stopped speaking to him for fear of it being misunderstood. Isn't that a shame? I actually avoided him the other day when I might've passed him in the hall. He doesn't understand why. I noticed you didn't come to me for confession.

SISTER JAMES: No. I went to Monsignor Benedict. He's very kind.

FLYNN: I wasn't?

SISTER JAMES: It wasn't that. As you know. You know why.

FLYNN: You're against me?

SISTER JAMES: No.

FLYNN: You're not convinced?

SISTER JAMES: It's not for me to be convinced, one way or the other. It's Sister Aloysius.

FLYNN: Are you just an extension of her?

SISTER JAMES: She's my superior.

FLYNN: But what about you?

SISTER JAMES: I wish I knew nothing whatever about it. I wish the idea had never entered my mind.

FLYNN: How did it enter your mind?

SISTER JAMES: Sister Aloysius.

FLYNN: I feel as if my reputation has been damaged through no fault of my own. But I'm reluctant to take the steps necessary to repair it for fear of doing further harm. It's frustrating, I can tell you that.

SISTER JAMES: Is it true?

FLYNN: What?

SISTER JAMES: You know what I'm asking.

FLYNN: No, it's not true.

SISTER JAMES: Oh, I don't know what to believe.

FLYNN: How can you take sides against me?

SISTER JAMES: It doesn't matter.

FLYNN: It does matter! I've done nothing. There's no substance to any of this. The most innocent actions can appear sinister to the poisoned mind. I had to throw that poor boy off the altar. He's devastated. The only reason I haven't gone to the monsignor is I don't want to tear apart the school. Sister Aloysius would most certainly lose her position as principal if I made her accusations known. Since they're baseless. You might lose your place as well.

SISTER JAMES: Are you threatening me?

FLYNN: What do you take me for? No.

SISTER JAMES: I want to believe you.

FLYNN: Then do. It's as simple as that.

SISTER JAMES: It's not me that has to be convinced.

FLYNN: I don't have to prove anything to her.

SISTER JAMES: She's determined.

FLYNN: To what?

SISTER JAMES: Protect the boy.

FLYNN: It's me that cares about that boy, not her. Has she ever reached out a hand to that child or any child in this school? She's like a block of ice! Children need warmth, kindness, understanding! What does she give them? Rules. That black boy needs a helping hand or he's not going to make it here! But if she has her way, he'll be left to his own undoing. Why do you think he was in the sacristy drinking wine that day? He's in trouble! She sees me talk in a human way to these children and she immediately assumes there must be something wrong with it. Something dirty. Well, I'm not going to let her keep this parish in the Dark Ages! And I'm not going to let her destroy my spirit of compassion!

SISTER JAMES: I'm sure that's not her intent.

FLYNN: I care about this congregation!

SISTER JAMES: I know you do.

FLYNN: Like you care about your class! You love them, don't you?

SISTER JAMES: Yes.

FLYNN: That's natural. How else would you relate to children? I can look at your face and know your philosophy: kindness.

SISTER JAMES: I don't know. I mean, of course.

FLYNN: What is Sister Aloysius's philosophy do you suppose?

(A pause.)

SISTER JAMES: I don't have to suppose. She's told me. She discourages . . . warmth. She's suggested I be more . . . formal.

FLYNN: There are people who go after your humanity, Sister James, who tell you the light in your heart is a weakness. That your soft feelings betray you. I don't believe that. It's an old tactic of cruel people to kill kindness in the name of virtue. Don't believe it. There's nothing wrong with love.

SISTER JAMES: Of course not, but . . .

FLYNN: Have you forgotten that was the message of the Savior to us all. Love. Not suspicion, disapproval and judgment. Love of people. Have you found Sister Aloysius a positive inspiration?

SISTER JAMES: I don't want to misspeak, but no. She's taken away my joy of teaching. And I loved teaching more than anything. *(She cries a little. He pats her uneasily, looking around)*

FLYNN: It's all right. You're going to be all right.

SISTER JAMES: I feel as if everything is upside down.

FLYNN: It isn't though. There are just times in life when we feel lost. You're not alone with it. It happens to many of us.

SISTER JAMES: A bond. *(Becomes self-conscious)* I'd better go in.

FLYNN: I'm sorry your brother is ill.

SISTER JAMES: Thank you, Father. *(Starts to go, stops)* I don't believe it!

FLYNN: You don't?

SISTER JAMES: No.

FLYNN: Thank you, Sister. That's a great relief to me. Thank you very much.

(She goes. He takes out his little black book and writes in it. The crow caws. He yells at it:)

Oh, be quiet.

(Then he opens a prayer book and walks away.)

VIII

Crossfade to the principal's office. Sister Aloysius is sitting looking out the window, very still. A knock at the door. She doesn't react. A second knock, louder. She pulls a small earplug out of her ear and scurries to the door. She opens it. There stands Mrs. Muller, a black woman of about thirty-eight, in her Sunday best, dressed for church. She's on red alert.

SISTER ALOYSIUS: Mrs. Muller?

MRS. MULLER: Yes.

SISTER ALOYSIUS: Come in.

(Sister Aloysius closes the door.)

Please have a seat.

MRS. MULLER: I thought I might a had the wrong day when you didn't answer the door.

SISTER ALOYSIUS: Oh. Yes. Well, just between us, I was listening to a transistor radio with an earpiece.

(She shows Mrs. Muller a very small transistor radio.)

Look at how tiny they're making them now. I confiscated it from one of the students and now I can't stop using it.

MRS. MULLER: You like music?

SISTER ALOYSIUS: Not really. News reports. Years ago I used to listen to all the news reports because my husband was in Italy in the war. When I came into possession of this little radio, I found myself doing it again. Though there is no war and the voices have changed.

MRS. MULLER: You were a married woman?

SISTER ALOYSIUS: Yes. But then he was killed. Is your husband coming?

MRS. MULLER: Couldn't get off work.

SISTER ALOYSIUS: I see. Of course. It was a lot to ask.

MRS. MULLER: How's Donald doing?

SISTER ALOYSIUS: He's passing his subjects. He has average grades.

MRS. MULLER: Oh. Good. He was upset about getting taken off the altar boys.

SISTER ALOYSIUS: Did he explain why?

MRS. MULLER: He said he was caught drinking wine.

SISTER ALOYSIUS: That is the reason.

MRS. MULLER: Well, that seems fair. But he's a good boy, Sister. He fell down there, but he's a good boy pretty much down the line. And he knows what an opportunity he has here. I think the whole thing was just a bit much for him.

SISTER ALOYSIUS: What do you mean, the whole thing?

MRS. MULLER: He's the only colored here. He's the first in this school. That'd be a lot for a boy.

SISTER ALOYSIUS: I suppose it is. But he has to do the work of course.

MRS. MULLER: He is doing it though, right?

SISTER ALOYSIUS: Yes. He's getting by. He's getting through. How is he at home?

MRS. MULLER: His father beat the hell out of him over that wine.

SISTER ALOYSIUS: He shouldn't do that.

MRS. MULLER: You don't tell my husband what to do. You just stand back. He didn't want Donald to come here.

SISTER ALOYSIUS: Why not?

MRS. MULLER: Thought he'd have a lot of trouble with the other boys. But that hasn't really happened as far as I can make out.

SISTER ALOYSIUS: Good.

MRS. MULLER: That priest, Father Flynn, been watching out for him.

SISTER ALOYSIUS: Yes. Have you met Father Flynn?

MRS. MULLER: Not exactly, no. I seen him on the altar, but I haven't met him face to face. No. Just, you know, heard from Donald.

SISTER ALOYSIUS: What does he say?

MRS. MULLER: You know, Father Flynn, Father Flynn. He looks up to him. The man gives him his time, which is what the boy needs. He needs that.

SISTER ALOYSIUS: Mrs. Muller, we may have a problem.

MRS. MULLER: Well, I thought you must a had a reason for asking me to come in. Principal's a big job. If you stop your day to talk to me, must be something. I just want to say though, it's just till June.

SISTER ALOYSIUS: Excuse me?

MRS. MULLER: Whatever the problem is, Donald just has to make it here till June. Then he's off into high school.

SISTER ALOYSIUS: Right.

MRS. MULLER: If Donald can graduate from here, he has a better chance of getting into a good high school. And that would mean an opportunity at college. I believe he has the intelligence. And he wants it, too.

SISTER ALOYSIUS: I don't see anything at this time standing in the way of his graduating with his class.

MRS. MULLER: Well, that's all I care about. Anything else is all right with me.

SISTER ALOYSIUS: I doubt that.

MRS. MULLER: Try me.

SISTER ALOYSIUS: I'm concerned about the relationship between Father Flynn and your son.

MRS. MULLER: You don't say. Concerned. What do you mean, concerned?

SISTER ALOYSIUS: That it may not be right.

MRS. MULLER: Uh-huh. Well, there's something wrong with everybody, isn't that so? Got to be forgiving.

SISTER ALOYSIUS: I'm concerned, to be frank, that Father Flynn may have made advances on your son.

MRS. MULLER: *May* have made.

SISTER ALOYSIUS: I can't be certain.

MRS. MULLER: No evidence?

SISTER ALOYSIUS: No.

MRS. MULLER: Then maybe there's nothing to it?

SISTER ALOYSIUS: I think there is something to it.

MRS. MULLER: Well, I would prefer not to see it that way if you don't mind.

SISTER ALOYSIUS: I can understand that this is hard to hear. I think Father Flynn gave Donald that altar wine.

MRS. MULLER: Why would he do that?

SISTER ALOYSIUS: Has Donald been acting strangely?

MRS. MULLER: No.

SISTER ALOYSIUS: Nothing out of the ordinary?

MRS. MULLER: He's been himself.

SISTER ALOYSIUS: All right.

MRS. MULLER: Look, Sister, I don't want any trouble, and I feel like you're on the march somehow.

SISTER ALOYSIUS: I'm not sure you completely understand.

MRS. MULLER: I think I understand the kind of thing you're talking about. But I don't want to get into it.

SISTER ALOYSIUS: What's that?

MRS. MULLER: Not to be disagreeing with you, but if we're talking about something floating around between this priest and my son, that ain't my son's fault.

SISTER ALOYSIUS: I'm not suggesting it is.

MRS. MULLER: He's just a boy.

SISTER ALOYSIUS: I know.

MRS. MULLER: Twelve years old. If somebody should be taking blame for anything, it should be the man, not the boy.

SISTER ALOYSIUS: I agree with you completely.

MRS. MULLER: You're agreeing with me but I'm sitting in the principal's office talking about my son. Why isn't the priest in the principal's office, if you know what I'm saying and you'll excuse my bringing it up.

SISTER ALOYSIUS: You're here because I'm concerned about Donald's welfare.

MRS. MULLER: You think I'm not?

SISTER ALOYSIUS: Of course you are.

MRS. MULLER: Let me ask you something. You honestly think that priest gave Donald that wine to drink?

SISTER ALOYSIUS: Yes, I do.

MRS. MULLER: Then how come my son got kicked off the altar boys if it was the man that gave it to him?

SISTER ALOYSIUS: The boy got caught, the man didn't.

MRS. MULLER: How come the priest didn't get kicked off the priesthood?

SISTER ALOYSIUS: He's a grown man, educated. And he knows what's at stake. It's not so easy to pin someone like that down.

MRS. MULLER: So you give my son the whole blame. No problem my son getting blamed and punished. That's easy. You know why that is?

SISTER ALOYSIUS: Perhaps you should let me talk. I think you're getting upset.

MRS. MULLER: That's because that's the way it is. You're just finding out about it, but that's the way it is and the way it's been, Sister. You're not going against no *man* in a *robe* and win, Sister. He's got the position.

SISTER ALOYSIUS: And he's got your son.

MRS. MULLER: Let him have 'im then.

SISTER ALOYSIUS: What?

MRS. MULLER: It's just till June.

SISTER ALOYSIUS: Do you know what you're saying?

MRS. MULLER: Know more about it than you.

SISTER ALOYSIUS: I believe this man is creating or has already brought about an improper relationship with your son.

MRS. MULLER: I don't know.

SISTER ALOYSIUS: I know I'm right.

MRS. MULLER: Why you need to know something like that for sure when you don't? Please, Sister. You got some kind a righteous cause going with this priest and now you want to drag my boy into it. My son doesn't need additional difficulties. Let him take the good and leave the rest when he leaves this place in June. He knows how to do that. I taught him how to do that.

SISTER ALOYSIUS: What kind of mother are you?

MRS. MULLER: Excuse me, but you don't know enough about life to say a thing like that, Sister.

SISTER ALOYSIUS: I know enough.

MRS. MULLER: You know the rules maybe, but that don't cover it.

SISTER ALOYSIUS: I know what I won't accept!

MRS. MULLER: You accept what you gotta accept and you work with it. That's the truth I know. Sorry to be so sharp, but you're in here in this room . . .

SISTER ALOYSIUS: This man is in my school.

MRS. MULLER: Well, he's gotta be somewhere and maybe he's doing some good too. You ever think of that?

SISTER ALOYSIUS: He's after the boys.

MRS. MULLER: Well, maybe some of them boys want to get caught. Maybe what you don't know maybe is my son is . . . that way. That's why his father beat him up. Not the wine. He beat Donald for being what he is.

SISTER ALOYSIUS: What are you telling me?

MRS. MULLER: I'm his mother. I'm talking about his nature now, not anything he's done. But you can't hold a child responsible for what God gave him to be.

SISTER ALOYSIUS: Listen to me with care, Mrs. Muller. I'm only interested in actions. It's hopeless to discuss a child's possible inclination. I'm finding it difficult enough to address a man's deeds. This isn't about what the boy may be, but what the man is. It's about the man.

MRS. MULLER: But there's the boy's nature.

SISTER ALOYSIUS: Let's leave that out of it.

MRS. MULLER: Forget it then. You're the one forcing people to say these things out loud. Things are in the air and you leave them alone if you can. That's what I know. My boy came to this school 'cause they were gonna kill him at the public school. So we were lucky enough to get him in here for his last year. Good. His father don't like him. He comes here, the kids don't like him. One man is good to him. This priest. Puts out a hand to the boy. Does the man have his reasons? Yes. Everybody has their reasons. *You* have your reasons. But do I ask the man why he's good to my son? No. I don't care why. My son needs some man to care about him and see him through to where he wants to go. And thank God, this educated man with some kindness in him wants to do just that.

SISTER ALOYSIUS: This will not do.

MRS. MULLER: It's just till June. Sometimes things aren't black and white.

SISTER ALOYSIUS: And sometimes they are. I'll throw your son out of this school. Make no mistake.

MRS. MULLER: But why would you do that? If nothing started with him?

SISTER ALOYSIUS: Because I will stop this whatever way I must.

MRS. MULLER: You'd hurt my son to get your way?

SISTER ALOYSIUS: It won't end with your son. There will be others, if there aren't already.

MRS. MULLER: Throw the priest out then.

SISTER ALOYSIUS: I'm trying to do just that.

MRS. MULLER: Well, what do you want from me?

(A pause.)

SISTER ALOYSIUS: Nothing. As it turns out. I was hoping you might know something that would help me, but it seems you don't.

MRS. MULLER: Please leave my son out of this. My husband would kill that child over a thing like this.

SISTER ALOYSIUS: I'll try.

(*Mrs. Muller stands up.*)

MRS. MULLER: I don't know, Sister. You may think you're doing good, but the world's a hard place. I don't know that you and me are on the same side. I'll be standing with my son and those who are good with my son. It'd be nice to see you there. Nice talking with you, Sister. Good morning.

(*She goes, leaving the door open behind her. Sister Aloysius is shaken. After a moment, Father Flynn appears at the door. He's in a controlled fury.*)

FLYNN: May I come in?
SISTER ALOYSIUS: We would require a third party.
FLYNN: What was Donald's mother doing here?
SISTER ALOYSIUS: We were having a chat.
FLYNN: About what?
SISTER ALOYSIUS: A third party is truly required, Father.
FLYNN: No, Sister. No third party. You and me are due for a talk.

(*He comes in and slams the door behind him. They face each other.*)

You have to stop this campaign against me!
SISTER ALOYSIUS: You can stop it at any time.
FLYNN: How?
SISTER ALOYSIUS: Confess and resign.
FLYNN: You are attempting to destroy my reputation! But the result of all this is going to be your removal, not mine!
SISTER ALOYSIUS: What are you doing in this school?

FLYNN: I am trying to do good!

SISTER ALOYSIUS: Or even more to the point, what are you doing in the priesthood?

FLYNN: You are single-handedly holding this school and this parish back!

SISTER ALOYSIUS: From what?

FLYNN: Progressive education and a welcoming church.

SISTER ALOYSIUS: You can't distract me, Father Flynn. This isn't about my behavior, it's about yours.

FLYNN: It's about your unfounded suspicions.

SISTER ALOYSIUS: That's right. I have suspicions.

FLYNN: You know what I haven't understood through all this? *Why* do you suspect me? What have I done?

SISTER ALOYSIUS: You gave that boy wine to drink. And you let him take the blame.

FLYNN: That's completely untrue! Did you talk to Mr. McGinn?

SISTER ALOYSIUS: All McGinn knows is the boy drank wine. He doesn't how he came to drink it.

FLYNN: Did his mother have something to add to that?

SISTER ALOYSIUS: No.

FLYNN: So that's it. There's nothing there.

SISTER ALOYSIUS: I'm not satisfied.

FLYNN: Well, if you're not satisfied, ask the boy then!

SISTER ALOYSIUS: No, he'd protect you. That's what he's been doing.

FLYNN: Oh, and why would he do that?

SISTER ALOYSIUS: Because you have seduced him.

FLYNN: You're insane! You've got it in your head that I've corrupted this child after giving him wine, and nothing I say will change that.

SISTER ALOYSIUS: That's right.

FLYNN: But correct me if I'm wrong. This has nothing to do with the wine, not really. You had a fundamental mis-

trust of me before this incident! It was you that warned
Sister James to be on the lookout, wasn't it?

SISTER ALOYSIUS: That's true.

FLYNN: So you admit it!

SISTER ALOYSIUS: Certainly.

FLYNN: Why?

SISTER ALOYSIUS: I know people.

FLYNN: That's not good enough!

SISTER ALOYSIUS: It won't have to be.

FLYNN: How's that?

SISTER ALOYSIUS: You will tell me what you've done.

FLYNN: Oh I will?

SISTER ALOYSIUS: Yes.

FLYNN: I'm not one of your truant boys, you know. Sister
James is convinced I'm innocent.

SISTER ALOYSIUS: So you talked to Sister James? Well, of
course you talked to Sister James.

FLYNN: Did you know that Donald's father beats him?

SISTER ALOYSIUS: Yes.

FLYNN: And might that not account for the odd behavior
Sister James noticed in the boy?

SISTER ALOYSIUS: It might.

FLYNN: Then what is it? What? What did you hear, what did
you see that convinced you so thoroughly?

SISTER ALOYSIUS: What does it matter?

FLYNN: I want to know.

SISTER ALOYSIUS: On the first day of the school year, I saw you
touch William London's wrist. And I saw him pull away.

FLYNN: That's all?

SISTER ALOYSIUS: That was all.

FLYNN: But that's nothing.

(He writes in his book.)

SISTER ALOYSIUS: What are you writing now?

FLYNN: You leave me no choice. I'm writing down what you say. I tend to get too flustered to remember the details of an upsetting conversation, and this may be important. When I talk to the monsignor and explain why you have to be removed as the principal of this school.

SISTER ALOYSIUS: This morning, before I spoke with Mrs. Muller, I took the precaution of calling the last parish to which you were assigned.

FLYNN: What did he say?

SISTER ALOYSIUS: Who?

FLYNN: The pastor?

SISTER ALOYSIUS: I did not speak to the pastor. I spoke to one of the nuns.

FLYNN: You should've spoken to the pastor.

SISTER ALOYSIUS: I spoke to a nun.

FLYNN: That's not the proper route for you to have taken, Sister! The Church is very clear. You're supposed to go through the pastor.

SISTER ALOYSIUS: Why? Do you have an understanding, you and he? Father Flynn, you have a history.

FLYNN: You have no right to go rummaging through my past!

SISTER ALOYSIUS: This is your third parish in five years.

FLYNN. Call the pastor and ask him why I left! It was perfectly innocent.

SISTER ALOYSIUS: I'm not calling the pastor.

FLYNN: I am a good priest! And there is nothing in my record to suggest otherwise.

SISTER ALOYSIUS: You will go after another child and another, until you are stopped.

FLYNN: What nun did you speak to?

SISTER ALOYSIUS: I won't say.

FLYNN: I've not touched a child.

SISTER ALOYSIUS: You have.

FLYNN: You have not the slightest proof of anything.

SISTER ALOYSIUS: But I have my certainty, and armed with that, I will go to your last parish, and the one before that if necessary. I will find a parent, Father Flynn! Trust me I will. A parent who probably doesn't know that you are *still working with children!* And once I do that, you will be exposed. You may even be attacked, metaphorically or otherwise.

FLYNN: You have no right to act on your own! You are a member of a religious order. You have taken vows, obedience being one! You answer to us! You have no right to step outside the Church!

SISTER ALOYSIUS: I will step outside the Church if that's what needs to be done, though the door should shut behind me! I will do what needs to be done, Father, if it means I'm damned to Hell! You should understand that, or you will mistake me. Now, did you give Donald Muller wine to drink?

FLYNN: Have you never done anything wrong?

SISTER ALOYSIUS: I have.

FLYNN: Mortal sin?

SISTER ALOYSIUS: Yes.

FLYNN: And?

SISTER ALOYSIUS: I confessed it! Did you give Donald Muller wine to drink?

FLYNN: Whatever I have done, I have left in the healing hands of my confessor. As have you! We are the same!

SISTER ALOYSIUS: We are not the same! A dog that bites is a dog that bites! I do not justify what I do wrong and go on. I admit it, desist, and take my medicine. Did you give Donald Muller wine to drink?

FLYNN: No.

SISTER ALOYSIUS: Mental reservation?

FLYNN: No.

SISTER ALOYSIUS: You lie. Very well then. If you won't leave my office, I will. And once I go, I will not stop.

(She goes to the door. Suddenly, a new tone comes into his voice.)

FLYNN: Wait!

SISTER ALOYSIUS: You will request a transfer from this parish. You will take a leave of absence until it is granted.

FLYNN: And do what for the love of God? My life is here.

SISTER ALOYSIUS: Don't.

FLYNN: Please! Are we people? Am I a person flesh and blood like you? Or are we just ideas and convictions. I can't say everything. Do you understand? There are things I can't say. Even if you can't imagine the explanation, Sister, remember that there are circumstances beyond your knowledge. Even if you feel certainty, it is an emotion and not a fact. In the spirit of charity, I appeal to you. On behalf of my life's work. You have to behave responsibly. I put myself in your hands.

SISTER ALOYSIUS: I don't want you.

FLYNN: My reputation is at stake.

SISTER ALOYSIUS: You can preserve your reputation.

FLYNN: If you say these things, I won't be able to do my work in the community.

SISTER ALOYSIUS: Your work in the community should be discontinued.

FLYNN: You'd leave me with nothing.

SISTER ALOYSIUS: That's not true. It's Donald Muller who has nothing, and you took full advantage of that.

FLYNN: I have not done anything wrong. I care about that boy very much.

SISTER ALOYSIUS: Because you smile at him and sympathize with him, and talk to him as if you were the same?

FLYNN: That child needed a friend!

SISTER ALOYSIUS: You are a cheat. The warm feeling you experienced when that boy looked at you with trust was not the sensation of virtue. It can be got by a drunkard from his tot of rum. You're a disgrace to the collar. The only reason you haven't been thrown out of the Church is the decline in vocations.

FLYNN: I can fight you.

SISTER ALOYSIUS: You will lose.

FLYNN: You can't know that.

SISTER ALOYSIUS: I know.

FLYNN: Where's your compassion?

SISTER ALOYSIUS: Nowhere you can get at it. Stay here. Compose yourself. Use the phone if you like. Good day, Father. I have no sympathy for you. I know you're invulnerable to true regret. *(Starts to go. Pause)* And cut your nails.

(She goes, closing the door behind her. After a moment, he goes to the phone and dials.)

FLYNN: Yes. This is Father Brendan Flynn of St. Nicholas parish. I need to make an appointment to see the bishop.

(Lights fade.)

IX

The lights crossfade to Sister Aloysius walking into the garden.
It's a sunny day. She sits on the bench. Sister James enters.

SISTER ALOYSIUS: How's your brother?

SISTER JAMES: Better. Much better.

SISTER ALOYSIUS: I'm very glad. I prayed for him.

SISTER JAMES: It was good to get away. I needed to see my family. It had been too long.

SISTER ALOYSIUS: Then I'm glad you did it.

SISTER JAMES: And Father Flynn is gone.

SISTER ALOYSIUS: Yes.

SISTER JAMES: Where?

SISTER ALOYSIUS: St. Jerome's.

SISTER JAMES: So you did it. You got him out.

SISTER ALOYSIUS: Yes.

SISTER JAMES: Donald Muller is heartbroken that he's gone.

SISTER ALOYSIUS: Can't be helped. It's just till June.

SISTER JAMES: I don't think Father Flynn did anything wrong.

SISTER ALOYSIUS: No? He convinced you?

SISTER JAMES: Yes, he did.

SISTER ALOYSIUS: Hmmm.

SISTER JAMES: Did you ever prove it?

SISTER ALOYSIUS: What?

SISTER JAMES: That he interfered with Donald Muller?

SISTER ALOYSIUS: Did I ever prove it to whom?

SISTER JAMES: Anyone but yourself?

SISTER ALOYSIUS: No.

SISTER JAMES: But you were sure.

SISTER ALOYSIUS: Yes.

SISTER JAMES: I wish I could be like you.

SISTER ALOYSIUS: Why?

SISTER JAMES: Because I can't sleep at night anymore. Everything seems uncertain to me.

SISTER ALOYSIUS: Maybe we're not supposed to sleep so well. They've made Father Flynn the pastor of St. Jerome.

SISTER JAMES: Who?

SISTER ALOYSIUS: The bishop appointed Father Flynn the pastor of St. Jerome Church and School. It's a promotion.

SISTER JAMES: You didn't tell them?

SISTER ALOYSIUS: I told our good Monsignor Benedict. I crossed the garden and told him. He did not believe it to be true.

SISTER JAMES: Then why did Father Flynn leave? What did you say to him to make him go?

SISTER ALOYSIUS: That I had called a nun in his previous parish. That I had found out his prior history of infringements.

SISTER JAMES: So you did prove it!

SISTER ALOYSIUS: I was lying. I made no such call.

SISTER JAMES: You lied?

SISTER ALOYSIUS: Yes. But if he had no such history, the lie wouldn't have worked. His resignation was his confession. He was what I thought he was. And he's gone.

SISTER JAMES: I can't believe you lied.

SISTER ALOYSIUS: In the pursuit of wrongdoing, one steps away from God. Of course there's a price.

SISTER JAMES: I see. So now he's in another school.

SISTER ALOYSIUS: Yes. Oh, Sister James!

SISTER JAMES: What is it, Sister?

SISTER ALOYSIUS: I have doubts! I have such doubts!

(Sister Aloysius is bent with emotion. Sister James comforts her. Lights fade.)

END OF PLAY

JOHN PATRICK SHANLEY is from the Bronx. He was thrown out of St. Helena's kindergarten. He was banned from St. Anthony's hot lunch program for life. He was expelled from Cardinal Spellman High School. He was placed on academic probation by New York University and instructed to appear before a tribunal if he wished to return. When asked why he had been treated in this way by all these institutions, he burst into tears and said he had no idea. Then he went into the United States Marine Corps. He did fine. He's still doing okay.